Copyright 2017 © Ka'ala Kaio Mahlangeni-Byndon.
All rights reserved. No part of this book may be used or reproduced by any means, graphic, electronic, or mechanical, including photocopying, recording, typing, or any information storage retrieval system without prior written permission of the author.

Written by Ka'ala Kaio Mahlangeni-Byndon
Cover and illustration by Bunch Ketty

For Aeva Lea, Kahealani, my future daughters, and little girls with afro crowns everywhere.

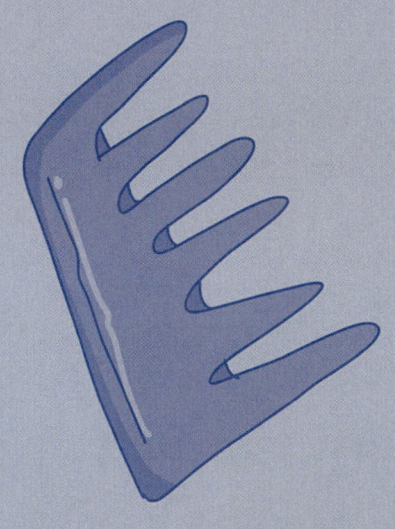
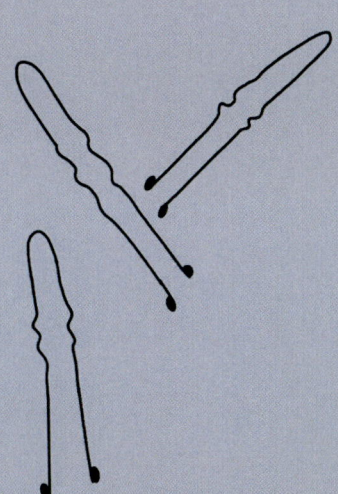

Sometimes I wear my crown in puffs.
They feel like clouds - soft and fluff.

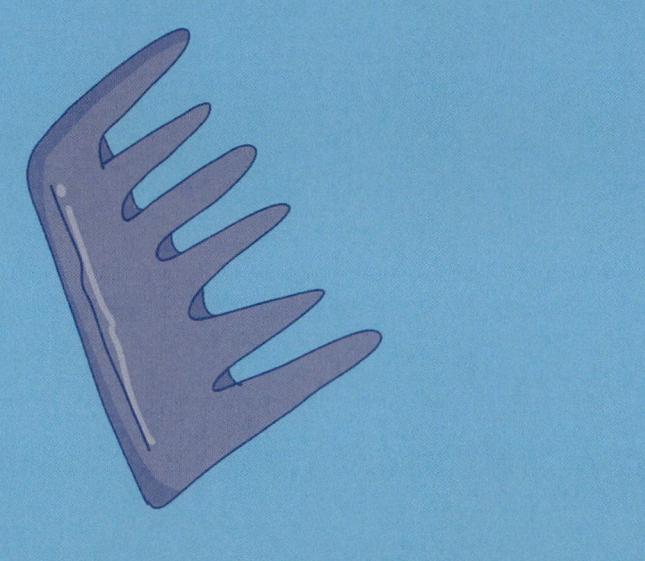

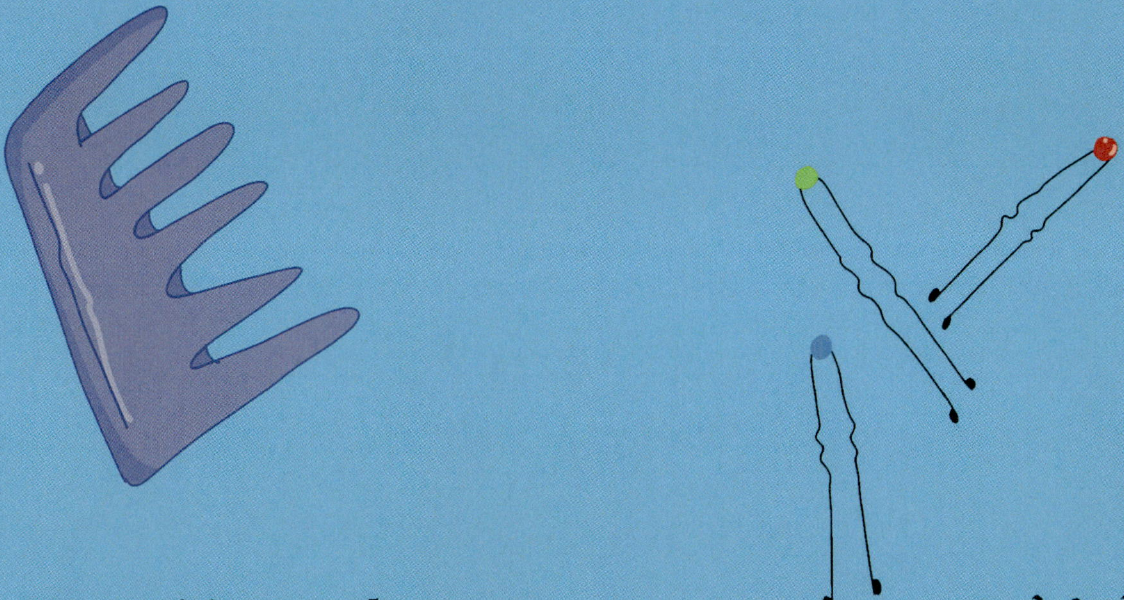

Sometimes I wear my crown up high.
I feel like my head can touch the sky.

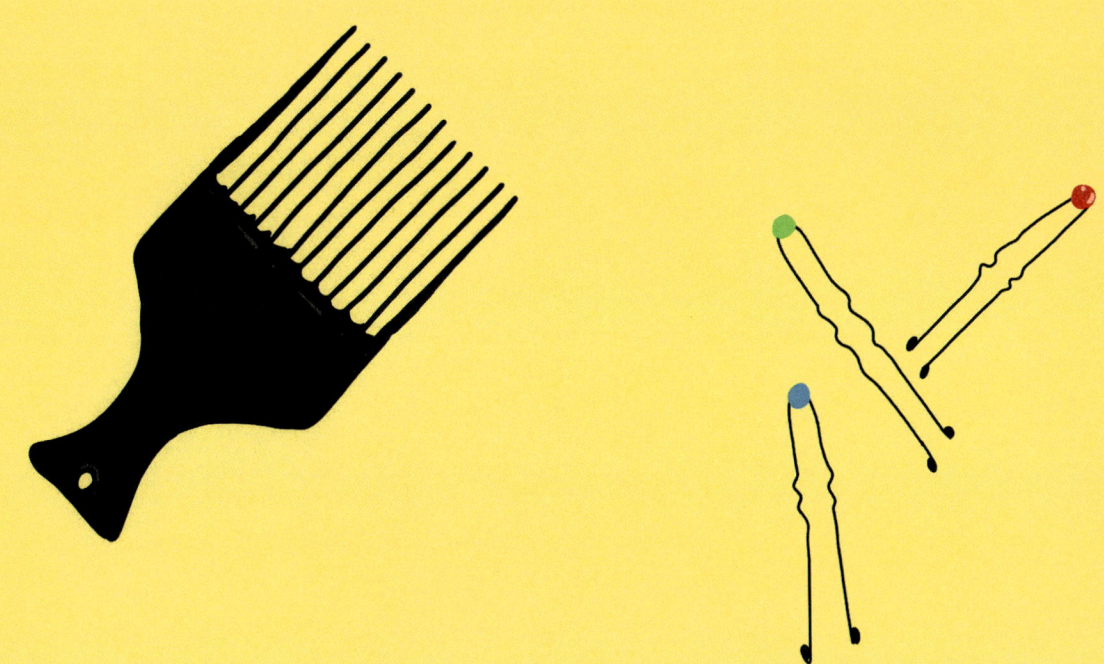

Sometimes I wear my crown wrapped up.
It makes my head feel tight and tucked.

Sometimes I wear my crown in twists.
They remind me of sweet licorice.

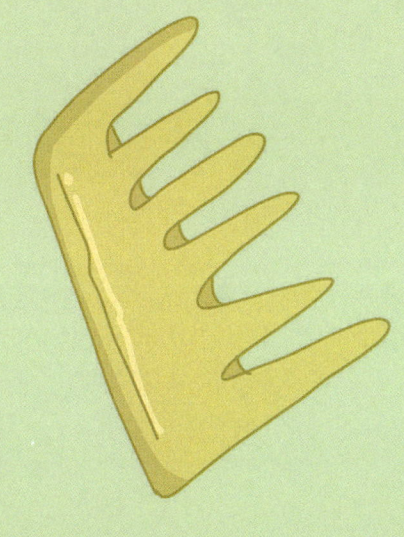
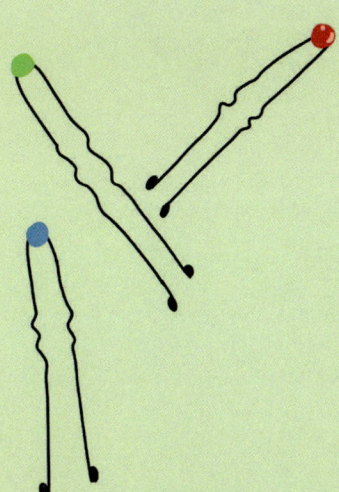

Sometimes I wear my crown with beads. They make fun sounds when they move in the breeze.

Sometimes I wear my crown straight.
It's nice and long and feels so great.

Sometimes I wear my crown with designs.
I have to be patient, it takes a long time.

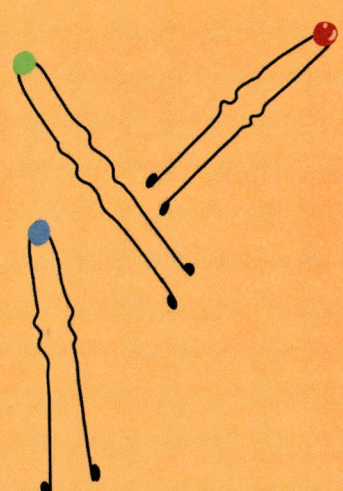

Sometimes I wear my crown in rows with braids and curls and sometimes bows.

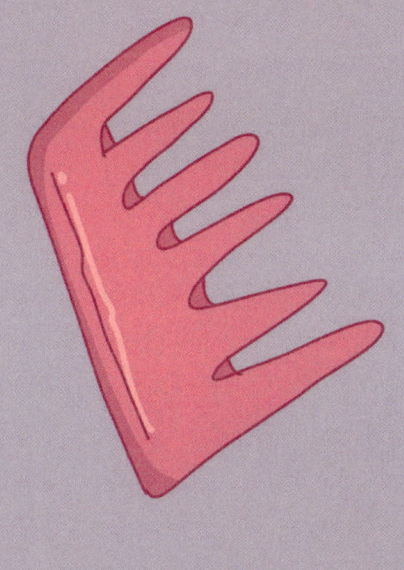
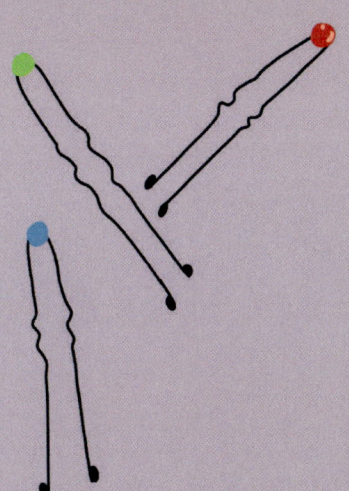

Someday I'll wear my crown in locs, just like my daddy rocks his locs.

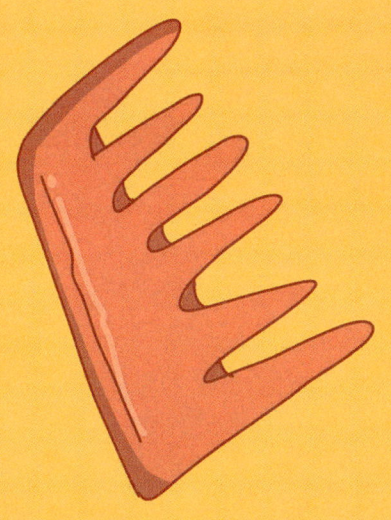
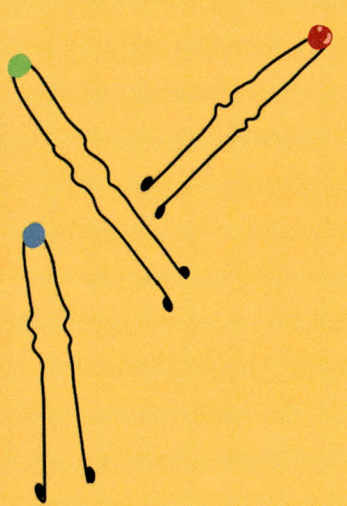

But my favorite way to wear my crown is natural - my afro - when I wear it down!

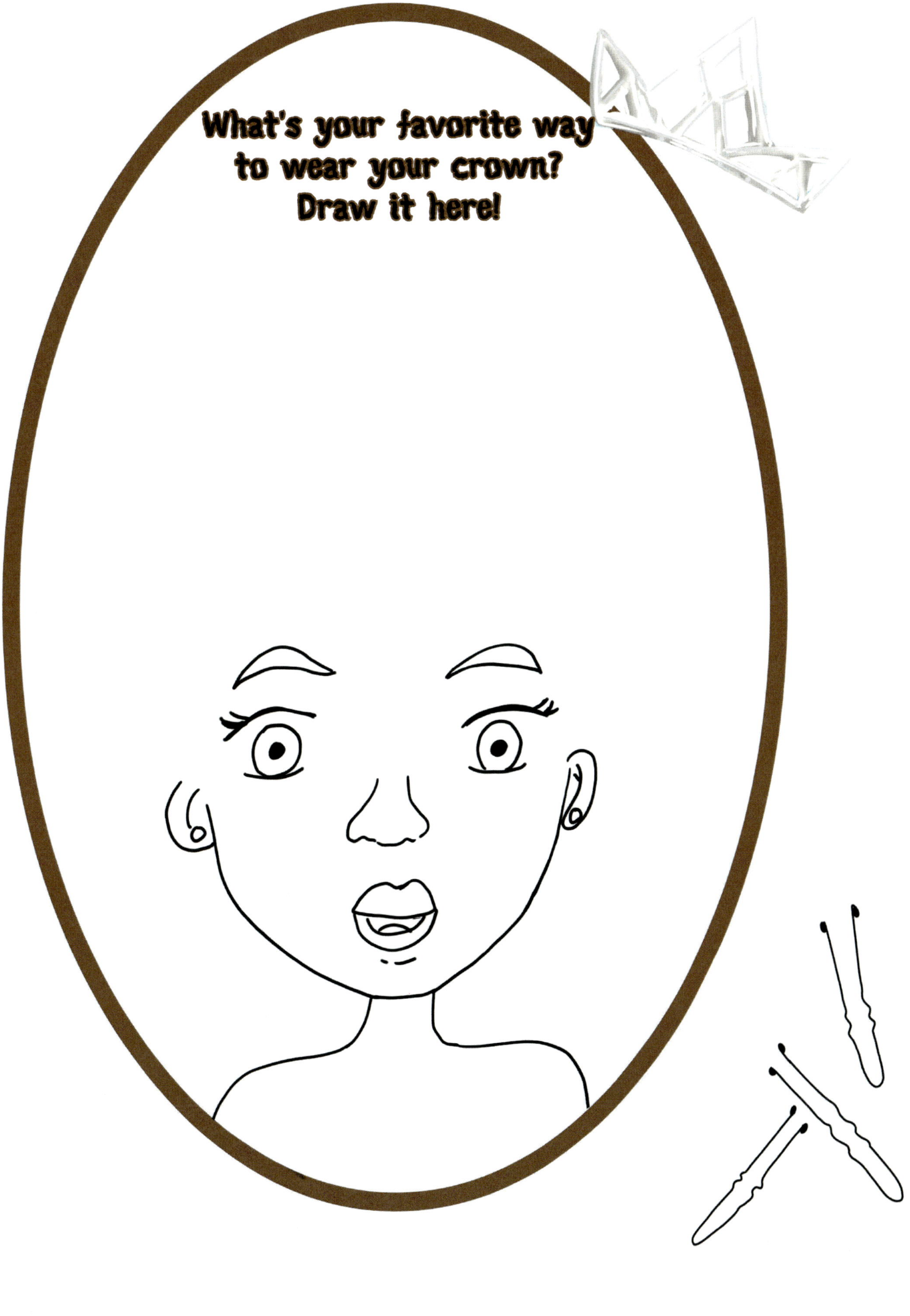
What's your favorite way
to wear your crown?
Draw it here!

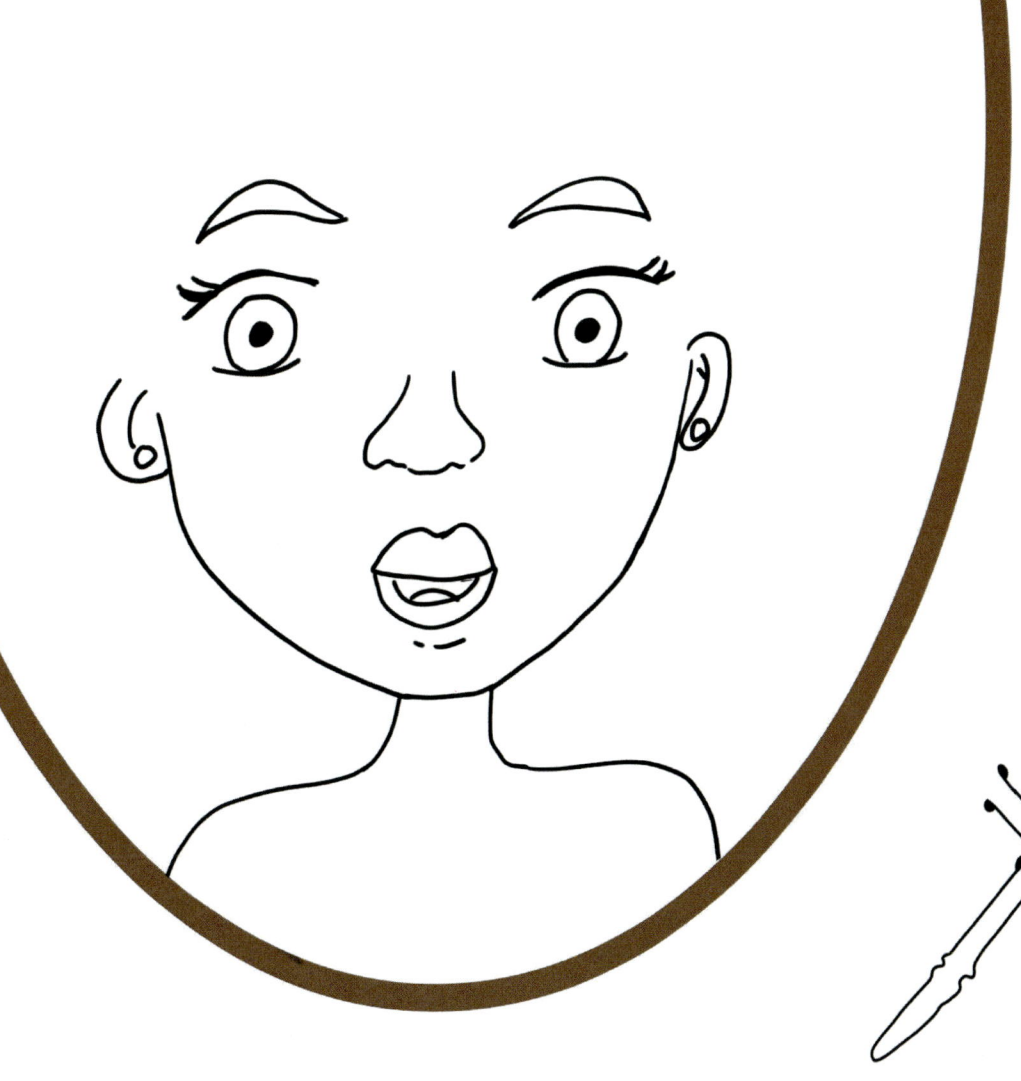

Author
Ka'ala Kaio Mahlangeni-Byndon

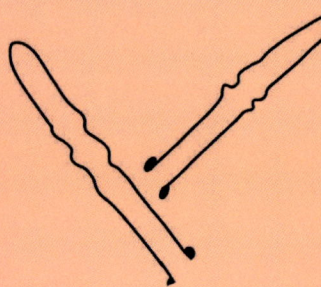

My name is Ka'ala Kaio Mahlangeni-Byndon. Yes, it is a long name! But I love it because those names make up who I am.
I am an island girl, born and raised on Maui.
A native Hawaiian beach baby. I married my best friend, Andile, who gave me my Xhosa last name.
Together we have diverse cultural roots, and share the same passion of educating others about the
significance of multiculturalism.

I am an educator, a musician, a writer, a jewelry maker, a wanderlust, and a child of God. My goal for this book is to inspire children to love the way they were created, embrace uniqueness, and recognize the beauty in the differences of others.

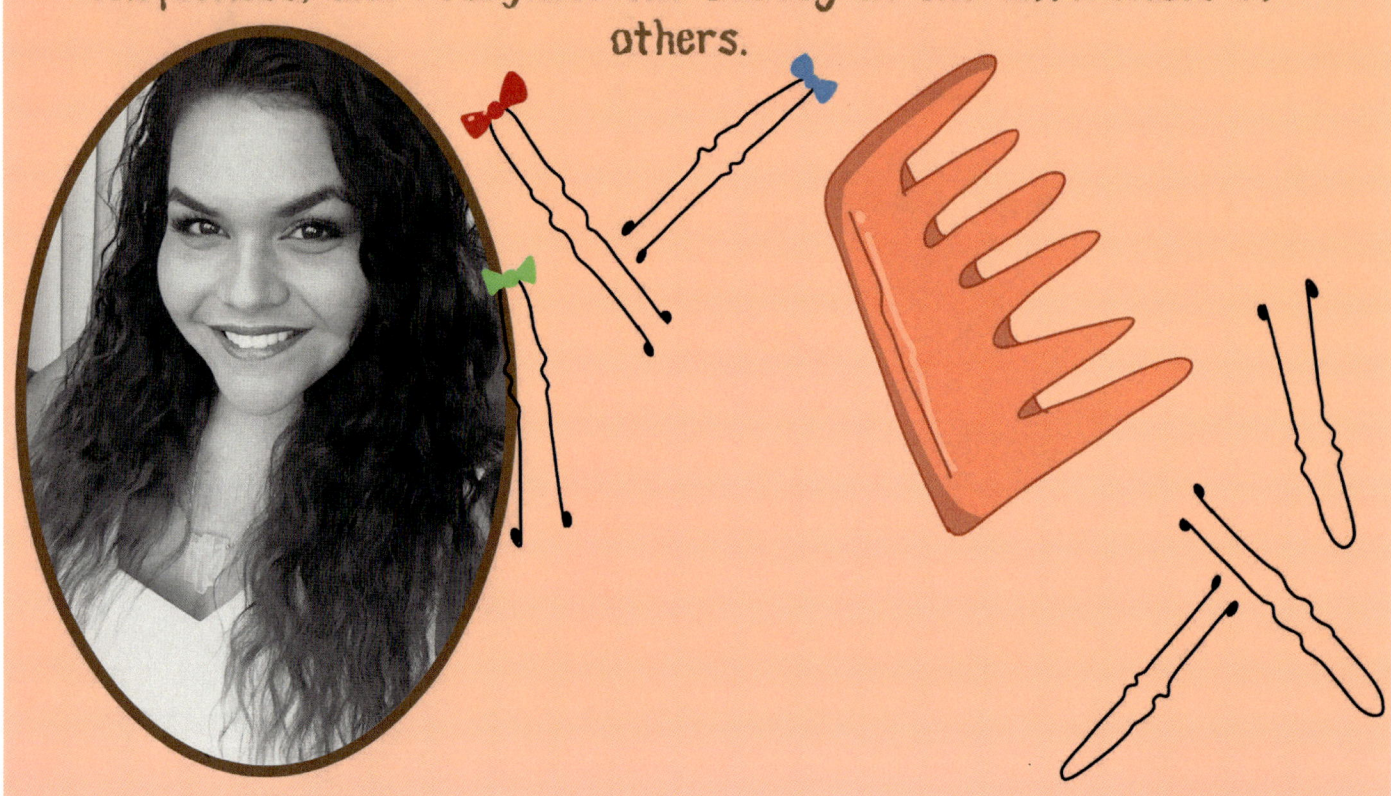

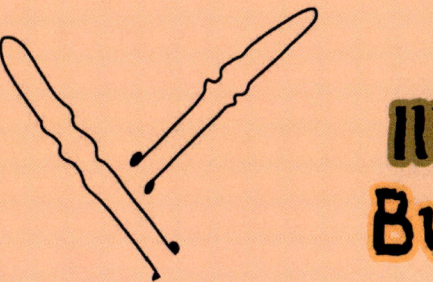

Illustrator
Bunch ketty

Hello.
I am a self-taught children's book illustrator.
A native of French Guiana.
I am the proud mother of a little six year old girl
with the sweet name of Kloaway.
I have drawn for as long as I can remember.
My drawing preference is for the world of kids
but I can adapt to different styles.
It's been over a year that I have had the opportunity
to work on projects emphasizing multiculturalism.

My works

Colette Market
Marake and Gold Seekers
Funny Parrot
Activity Book on Multiculturalism
My Best Friend Likes Boy More Than Me!

Contact: bunchketty@hotmail.com
Web: https://facebook.com/Tassussu
https:facebook.com/bunch.ketty
https://kettybunch.wordpress.com

Made in the USA
Monee, IL
03 June 2020